The Memory Theater Burned

The Memory Theater Burned

DAMON KRUKOWSKI

TURTLE POINT ❧ NEW YORK ❧ 2004

©2004 Damon Krukowski

Some of these poems were first published in
*Arsenal, The Boston Phoenix, Web Conjunctions, Faucheuse,
Grand Street,* and *The Impercipient Lecture Series.*
Grateful acknowledgment is made to the editors of those
publications: Olivier Brossard, Jon Garelick, Bradford Morrow,
Jeff Clark, Jean Stein and Deborah Treisman,
Steve Evans and Jennifer Moxley.

Book design by Naomi Yang

Turtle Point Press
233 Broadway, Room 946
New York, NY 10279

Distributed by DAP, Distributed Art Publishers
155 Avenue of the Americas, 2nd floor
New York, N.Y. 10013

ISBN: 1-885586-95-7
LIBRARY OF CONGRESS CONTROL NUMBER: 2003105379

Table of Contents

The Memory Theater Burned
{1}

The War ❧ Kaddish ❧ Economy ❧ Song Without Words ❧ Mute ❧ The Memory Theater Burned ❧ I Will Always Remember Primrose Hill ❧ First Sabbath ❧ The Copyist ❧ A Bowl of Lentils, A Dish of Game ❧ Raree Show ❧ The Analysand ❧ At the Café Detroit ❧ A Still, Small Voice ❧ The Longest Day ❧ A Testimonial ❧ Sonho de Valsa ❧ Venus and Neptune ❧ All the Fountains of the Great Deep Burst Apart ❧ Into the Medina ❧ My Life as the History of a Town ❧ Last Supper on the Shanghai Bund ❧ Dream ❧ The Virtuoso

Vexations
{37}

Vexations ❧ Bells ❧ A Misunderstanding ❧ The Envelope ❧ Reading ❧ In Private ❧

After the Tempest ❧ Sleep ❧ Read Me ❧ To Levitate ❧ Mildred Pierce ❧ The Extra ❧ The Secret Museum ❧ Hearts and Pearls ❧ Caresse Crosby Dreams a Dream ❧ Ghosts ❧ Mise en Abyme ❧ Only One Thing is Missing ❧ The Blue God ❧ Meditation ❧ A Parable ❧ The Argument ❧ The Image ❧ Poetry

The Memory Theater Burned

The War

When the war started my father began to dig a trench; at first we imagined it was a shelter for the family but he never tried to protect us in it. At the time the war was quite a distance away, and a shelter seemed unnecessary, though we respected father's precaution. As the trench grew deeper, its potential function became more obscure, however. It wasn't long before father had to build an elaborate scaffold to continue his work, with a maze of ladders to climb down in the morning, and back out at night. When he began to work in the dark as well, the light from his torches and smudge pots cast shadows into the sky that seemed anything but prudent, given the bombardments. Thankfully the bombs never fell that close to our town; nevertheless father continued digging, and even after the war had finally ended, continued to dig his trench. The neighbors had long since stopped speaking to him, and to mother, and even we children were regarded with suspicion, both by the town and by its new authorities. Eventually these authorities came to inspect the trench — which was now hardly a trench but more a construction of wood and stone as solid as if it had been a house above ground — and there was a time of uncertainty when we worried that father might be fined, or worse, as a result. But the authorities could find no laws, either extant under the previous regime or newly written by the nascent one, that applied to the structure and so, after the exchange of a few small bribes from my mother, left father to continue his work. Perhaps they realized that a man in a hole is no danger, at least not to anyone else. For the trench had become so large as to encompass my father's entire world. With the dangers of war removed, he took to staying in his trench at all hours of day and night. We could no longer determine whether he was still working on it, or had finally decided it was finished. Indeed, we never saw him again. The only evidence of his existence — the trench — was so deep and so narrow that it had swallowed up his presence. Eventually we covered the trench over, and said a prayer.

Kaddish

IN MOURNING FOR MYSELF, I did nothing for a year that reminded me of my personality. I read religious tracts (I am a non-believer); traveled the world (I am agoraphobic); wrote novels (I am inarticulate); and sang songs (I am tone deaf). At the end of the year, I mended my clothes and resumed my personality. But I was now a public figure, famous for my singing, my novels, my travels, and my spiritual inner life. My former self had died, and so I have returned into mourning.

Economy

I HAVE A limited number of words to speak or write. You might think that I would choose them carefully; but in fact I am quite garrulous. I do not worry about expressing my opinions too baldly; nor do I dance around a topic; or soften my feelings with attempts at elegant, decorous conversation. I am unafraid to run out of words, because all this communication has made me tired. I long for silence, for an end to the blistering insults I am compelled to dole out to all around me. That is what they are generally considered, these attempts at direct, truthful and economical communication. I do not know when I will run out of words. But when I do, please remember that I was once a free talker.

Song Without Words

My instrument is easy to play, and I played it for hours on end. People make a fuss at times, but really it is an easy instrument, and if I became especially proficient on it, it was only because it is so easy to play that I played it often. Eventually, for variety, I began to play the instrument in unusual ways; that is, I played different parts of the instrument than are typically used, and I used my body in new ways to play it. These were just small adjustments and inventions I introduced to amuse myself. Joyfully, I played the instrument with my whole body, stamping my feet, clapping my hands. And one day it occurred to me: If I play with my whole body, why do I not sing, too? So I began to sing while I played my instrument. I played, and I stomped and clapped, and I sang as well. But as I sang, I began to think of the words I was singing — these were simple words, both sad and happy ones I had picked up from different lullabies or folksongs

I remembered hearing in childhood. The words, though simple, began to affect me. I thought about them more and more often, and they began to take on greater import than I had at first realized. These phrases, taken at random from my memory in the midst of the joy of playing my instrument, began to trouble me. It seemed to me that I had pulled my very memory from my body, and flung it out into the road where I stomped and clapped, disrespectfully dancing across my own thoughts. My mind, emptied of these memories, became obsessed with them. I wanted to re-collect them, stuff them in again and forget them as thoroughly as I had before. But the memories, remembered, wouldn't go back. They were there every time I played my instrument, emerging from my voice. And as I played constantly, they were constantly there. I began to live only through these memories. My playing took on a dirge-like, mournful tone. People were saddened to hear me play. They crossed the street, or themselves, when they saw me coming — stomping, clapping, and yelling out my memories, the memories that were now forever before my face. Eventually, I could no longer play my instrument, easy as it is, while I sang. Singing was a struggle with my mind, and my body, always content to simply play my instrument, could not manage without my mind. Finally, I lost the ability to play my instrument. I picked it up as often as before, but my body wouldn't respond. I stood still, clutching my instrument, screaming the phrases that had jumped from the depths of my mind, which had nowhere else to go.

Never, no matter how easy your instrument, begin to sing.

Mute

I AM MUTE, ignored, covered in dust. At the end of a dark dry hallway, I sit high on a shelf and consider my position. Humble, to be sure. Pride left me when I entered this black building, unlit and cool like a tomb. No mute can cry out, but one more proud might rattle the bars, kick over the furniture. I despair at how readily I surrender, at my inability to complete projects once begun. There was a time, I believe, when I focused my energies and worked diligently to improve my situation. But this thought may be exaggerated by feelings of nostalgia; even misery is subject to nostalgia. At present, my mind is ill at ease, my concentration fractured, though there is nominally nothing here on which to concentrate. My only comfort is that you, if you think of me, will think of me in this miserable state. A comfort because at last I will have communicated something through the blackness of my isolation and silence.

The Memory Theater Burned

The memory theater burned, and in its ruins I could remember only portions of scripture, commentary, history, poetry, biographies of notable men, successful recipes, homeopathy, botany, and the classification of animals. I do not wish to fill the world with nonsense, but I cannot recall these pieces without supplying connective elements; and so I am constructing, anew, my own hybrid theater. Some of its niches are now supported by boulders or crude timbers. Some are covered in cloth so as to hide their ruination. I loved the theater, in its perfection; and I am pained to see it in fragments. But fragments are all I find, and what I find is all I can remember.

I Will Always Remember Primrose Hill
(a sheaf of wheat for mr. epstein)

Primrose Hill? If I tell you my view of it, will this help you find it? Places, like people, are witness to many things; but unlike people, they bear no responsibility for what they have seen. If a boy stands on a hill, and stands there until he becomes a man, does the hill change as well? The grass may show signs of his ceaseless presence; and other living things, the fauna, may adapt to his vigil. But this place — and it is just one place on earth — has no memory. And the man's memory of the hill, whatever it may be, is a part of the man; and when the man finally dies and sinks into the hill, his memory shall remain a part of the man and not of the hill.

And so we walked by Primrose Hill, never seeing it.

First Sabbath

I HAVE TWO EYES, so I give you one. I have two lungs, so I give you one. I have two hearts, so I give you one. I sneeze for good luck. Your spirit enters the room.

Strange knockings as the heating pipes expand, contract. It is the new moon, and the first frost. The Nephilim arrive, ready to cohabit for the winter.

The Copyist

I WRITE WITH the holy intent of writing. Because these may be the words of God: I am his creation and words are his gift. I write with my hands screening the page, because like the Sabbath candles, these words create both the occasion and the need for blessing. But what blessing can I speak, with words I cannot see and dare not say? To avoid possible error, I do not speak.

I write with the holy intent of writing. And if I fail to think, and can only copy out others' thoughts, at least I will have been a copyist.

A Bowl of Lentils, A Dish of Game

The desert is lush, in places. Who will sit in the sand, who on the heights? If there were enough for all, Jacob and Esau could sit together and eat, Esau grunting, Jacob watching. But watching leads to contemplation, internal debate, neurosis. Who am I to despise my brother, his hairy hands, his brutal ways, his careless words, his awful wives? Who am I but Jacob, son of the patriarchs. Who am I but Rebekah's son.

Raree Show

I AM THE PROMPTER at our national theater. It would be a good job, if the principal actor and actress were not my parents. What is more, they never forget their lines. Each performance, I stand and watch my parents embrace, quarrel, stab one another, and embrace again. They look my way rarely, and at each other never. They are our nation's greatest actor and actress because they love the audience more than they love one another, me, or even themselves. I sit six nights a week (and twice on Saturdays) in my prompter's box and read. Except I do not read, because I have already memorized every line in every play of our national theater. Many I had memorized before I came to my post as prompter; at the dining table these same lines were repeated endlessly. Once I wanted to be a writer. But I soon found that these lines were so ingrained in my memory, their path worn so smooth, any phrase I thought of would inevitably be followed by the next from some famous dialogue. I could only have been a plagiarist; or a prompter. The job of prompter utilizes my best ability — were I to employ this talent instead of wasting it — that is, memory. From the beginning of my consciousness I remember all that my parents have said, and done. True, they often repeat their actions, gestures, and words (what actor or actress does not?); but I can recall even the smallest variations in their hackneyed lives. Similarly, I recall each and every performance of the interminable plays that I witness each night. At home, after the performance, I drink heavily to erase this image of my parents, in full makeup and lit spectacularly by the footlights, prancing before me in that buzz of expectation that can only be generated by a thousand attentive minds. As prompter, I never see the audience, but I watch the stage with all their eyes.

The Analysand

I SHOWED THIS poem to my mother, and she said: This is not a poem, this is a story your grandfather told me...

I showed this poem to my mother, and she said: This is not a poem, this is a song I sang at Minton's...

I showed this poem to my mother, and she said: This is not a poem, this is a dream I had... Why did you read my dream book?

At the Café Detroit

THEY CAME TO ME and said, old man, we want you to sing your songs for us again, everyone has forgotten them. But I said: If everyone has forgotten them, how do you know you want to hear them? I am old and tired of singing for those who do not care. But they continued: We remember the subjects of the songs, we remember the feelings of the songs, we just cannot remember their details. Please sing us your songs again. But I said: If you remember the subjects and the feelings, that is enough, the rest is for an old man to take to his grave. But they protested: Old man, we loved your music when you were young, and we were children. Our parents loved your music, but now they are dead. We want our children to hear it. You must sing for us again. I was moved, but I knew what lay ahead, so still I resisted. I said: If you really loved my music, you would remember its details as well and not have to bother me in my old age, to recall such painful memories. Here they sensed more than they had known. But old man, they asked, can the songs that bring us joy bring you pain? (These were no longer children, but nonetheless young enough to ask such foolish questions.) I told them: I will not sing for you, but I will tell you my secret. With it you can sing songs yourself, and suffer through life until you too are an old man who no longer wants to sing. This is all I know: It is songs of pain that bring people joy. I am old and tired of pain. And you, who know no pain, can never bring me joy. So they let me be, at last.

A Still, Small Voice

THIS TIME, God sends Moses up a mountain to see the promised land, and die.

But in the Haftarah, we find Elijah on a mountain — on Sinai, the mountain of the law. And here Elijah hears the still, small voice of God. The voice asks, "What are you doing here, Elijah?"

Of course he had been commanded to be there.

We are given the law, we seek a higher law, we are visited by an angel, we are fortified by cakes and march for forty days, and up a mountain, the mountain of the law. Then, if we are the prophet Elijah, we are finally addressed, and the address is this question: "What are you doing here?"

Is this what Moses heard before he died?

The Longest Day

The longest day surprises us, having approached so slowly as to appear, from a distance, as if standing still. But suddenly it's 9:00, 9:30, even 10:00 PM, and the faint light in the sky announces its arrival. The next evening is bright, but already we see the back of day. The longest night approaches.

A Testimonial

I HAD A DREAM to record a nation's songs, a people's music, in its entirety. With such a document, it might be possible to catalogue all emotion; I even believed, in more giddy moments, that it might reveal all thought.

But what nation is both musical, and small enough to document thoroughly? In my search for an ideal subject, my own prejudices and tastes began to interfere: not all music, it seemed to me, was worthy of such an investigation. Could a theory of mind emerge from a mindless music?

I decided to invert the project, and record all the music I could think of myself. Might not one individual's music, if executed with honesty and discipline, reveal the same range of mind as a people's? Important questions were raised by such an assertion, but I lay them aside: to write and record this music I would need complete concentration and dedication of effort.

I sang directly into a tape recorder. My practice resembled certain rituals I have witnessed in my travels; after a prolonged period of singing without break, my mental state would approach euphoria, aided by disorientation, lack of food and water, and hyperventilation. I do not know how long I was recording because the tape often ran out without my noticing. I believe, from external evidence, that it may have been a month or more.

The body is capable of remarkable feats, when the mind is focused and the breath active. I drained myself of song, like a body of blood. Onto the tape I spilled out my consciousness; at times I was left a shell of myself, perhaps it was a state of madness, or of pure instinct such as we believe animals possess.

However, our most basic instinct is survival, and even this I eventually violated. The tapes I made are filled with screaming, as I frequently experienced pain from the privations required by my experiment. There are, I believe, more tapes of screaming than of singing. There may be no singing on them at all. I cannot say, because I have been unable to listen to these tapes. Empty of song, I have found that I am empty of desire. There is nothing left inside, and the external evidence I have created is only a mirror for this same nothing.

Sonho de Valsa

The earth might be a red paper ball, hanging by a thread in the center of a room lined with books. Through a gap in the books can be seen a man, his eyes meet yours. The ball is cut down, and it is clear that you must care for it. But how can you be both of this earth, and holding it delicately in your hands?

Venus and Neptune

Astrologists have long maintained that the planets each revealed themselves only when they were ready to be seen. Neptune, shrouded in mist and fog, was discovered in the 1840s, as Romanticism took its own damp form. Pluto, dark and stony, was first sighted in 1930, ushering in a cold age of Fascist evil. So perhaps it should not have come as such a surprise when the planets began to disappear. Pluto was the first to vanish, a blow to science but for many a great relief. Restored to its rotation of eight, the solar system seemed more elegant, Victorian, and high minded. But then Saturn, Uranus, Mars, Mercury, and finally the great Jupiter also vanished from the sky. Foggy Neptune and lovely Venus only remained. And so they shall, goes one popular theory, because many believe that Earth will be the next to go. Unobserved at last, Venus and Neptune will enjoy alone together the peace and ineffable beauty of the stars.

All the Fountains of the Great Deep Burst Apart

We are the eleventh generation; from the tenth only our fathers survive. Is it any wonder our language is confused? God heard us talking about our fathers, and confounded us.

The tenth generation had one, mythic language, because what they saw is beyond description.

What we know is unworthy of description. And for this we use words: confounded, rare and unique words.

Into the Medina

A BOY TOOK my hand and led me into the labyrinth of the medina. This was a dream, but only the boy knew its plan and I was helpless to leave it without him. I struggled through the press of the crowd to keep up with him. He slipped through people like water. We came to an open courtyard, filled with shops. Each shopkeeper beckoned to me, but the boy turned toward a closed door and I followed. He opened this door onto yet another street, more crowded than all the others, filled with spice vendors and carpenters, the air heavy with cedar resin and the thousand spices they mix together to make *ras el hanout*. The boy began to slip ahead, always more smoothly and silently, his body compressing like a cat. Clumsily I followed, bumping into passers-by, store displays, and bundles on the backs of donkeys. Exhausted, I fell into the doorway of a mosque. The boy appeared at my side. Together with an old man they bundled me onto the back of a donkey. The stench was unbearable; I was lying on a mat of uncured skins, meant for drums, or shoes, or another thousand products. The boy whistled to direct the donkey. We continued through the labyrinth. Am I dead and dreaming of a life, I thought, that consists of the medina, this boy, and a labyrinth of thoughts that cannot free themselves from the unknowable plan of these streets. Or am I alive and dreaming I am dead. Either way, I will never find my way out of the medina.

My Life as the History of a Town

THE TOWN GREW up along the river, but the river dried up. No one ever walks, or even steps, into the riverbed. The finest houses are built with a view of the river. Walking along its banks, one can see into the sumptuous rooms of these palaces. Above, one sees the sky in all its moods and variations. Bridges, made of wood, rot slowly and are replaced. Boats, immobile for generations, are carefully repaired and painted. Without the river, life in this town would be a dusty, airless hell.

Last Supper on the Shanghai Bund

The Last Supper wasn't a meal, but a meeting — a long table set out along the Bund, Shanghai, with its grand buildings behind, and the broad Nanjing Road stretching before it. My own feeling was of being trapped in the dense crowd that filled either side of the avenue. In the center was an open space; I held a white square of paper, and thought I might throw it across to help me reach the other side. But as it sailed over that space, it suddenly plummeted to the ground at the very center. I realized this was opposite Jesus, and it was his presence that had struck the paper down. This was the sign that would enable me to leave the press of the crowd and escape, both unnoticed and called apart.

Dream

Near escapes all day. From a town so small it is only one room, with slots in the walls for windows. We watch the planes pass overhead, but they will not stop here because this town is too small, it is only one room.

The Virtuoso

THE GUITAR GREW heavy, heavier each day. At first it was enough to shift my position while playing, but soon my legs began to ache from supporting its weight. When I couldn't bear it any longer on my lap, I began placing it on a low bench covered in cloth to protect the wood. On the third night of this arrangement, the bench collapsed. The guitar was undamaged; its mass had changed and the wood was now a denser material than the floor. It had become impossible to lift the guitar without assistance, and as I travel alone, I had no choice but to leave it where it lay. The nightclub allowed me to extend my gig, for the time being, so the next day I set to work learning how to play the guitar as it lay on the stage. I found a rug, and performed cross-legged, with the guitar before me. I could no longer move its neck. As its weight increased, the guitar began to sink into the floor. The next evening, I lay prone on the rug and stretched out my arms, reaching over the top of the instrument rather than from below. Eventually the guitar sank level with the stage. I lay down beside it now, no longer plucking or strumming its strings but simply stroking its wood. I found that I too was growing heavy, perhaps from the immobility of this new position. The next evening, I did not get up after my performance. All night, I lay beside the guitar, as we sank together deeper into the ground. I could see the lights of the room above me, as far away as the stars on a clear night. When these lights faded, the guitar and I entered a world I had heard about in myth and song, but which I had never believed I would witness. I did not see it, exactly, but felt it seep around us, and then inside us, making us ever heavier. Once it had filled us both completely, I could no longer find any difference between myself and the guitar.

Vexations

Vexations

When I first began to sing this song, I was inspired by feelings of love and beauty. But this song has continued long past its inspiration; I have been singing, continuously, for many years now, and my inspiration was — as it turned out — only momentary. This song is so familiar I can sing it somewhat automatically, while I accomplish other tasks such as eating, washing, and obviously writing this page. But what I cannot do is sing another song. I have been told that there are Tibetan monks who are able to sing two tunes simultaneously, but these monks must not sing a song such as I have been singing all these years. It takes the whole voice to sing this song; the mind can wander momentarily — it is remarkable how much can be accomplished in a moment — however the voice must be concentrated, indeed the whole body must participate to some degree. This is because this song is sung at top volume. It must be extremely loud.

This was an aspect of my initial inspiration, and I will never compromise that vision. It is a song that — for all its other defects, which I now know all too well — is incomparably, magnificently loud. I believe that it may be the loudest song ever composed, and if I am not the loudest singer who ever lived, I must rank fairly high among those that have gone before, as I have never met a louder singer in my lifetime. Some contend that it is difficult to compare, because other singers claim it is impossible to perform in my presence. They say that this is because of my continuous singing, but I believe it is simply egotism, a common fault of singers. It may be that I am typical in this regard. But my song, and its volume, are anything but typical. About this song: it is very simple, however it expresses all that I have just said. It also expresses my desire for it to end. But it is perpetual. I will die before this song ends, and then it will carry on without me — still at a deafening volume. There is no other way for this song to be sung.

Bells

Your ears are ringing; the tone is C#; the rain is falling. There are motors whirring everywhere, in the computer on which you type these thoughts; in the clock by the bed on which you read this page; in the bulb of the lamp with the halogen light, so compact and yet so much louder than light sources many thousands and millions times its size: the sun, for example. Which is not shining, or ringing, at the moment, but somewhere exploding in sight of a telescope which does not measure light but rather changes in the radio waves — buzzing — that everywhere envelop us.

There is no end to the ringing which began with the background radiation of the cosmos, which was at one time silent to you, but then rushed into your ears like salt water, pushing insistently and painfully against the small space beside your eardrum, broadcasting its confused message out for anyone capable of understanding it to receive: two people, one male and one female, holding hands, the man gesturing with his other arm as if to say hello, but who knows what one upraised hand might mean? You would have rather placed that hand cupped to one ear, listening, as if you didn't hear enough already, to other messages broadcast across the skies.

Which are shrill with airplanes, helicopters, office towers packed with air conditioners and topped by enormous weights and pulleys for elevators, and then higher up satellites, space stations, and colliding junk, not to mention asteroids, dust, and the shaking harmony of the spheres themselves.

No dream was ever so noisy as this, which wakes you breathless from sleep; it's the familiar dream of bees swarming across a field, you see the field in daylight yet the scene is dark, lit by the half-light of the midnight sun. Bees swarm around your head, singing a song of only one note — C# — which you recognize as the last note anyone will hear, because the world is running out of air, and air conveys sound. The bees are ignorant of the silence they violate. Then the field is in true darkness, the bees are gone, there is no sound except the memory of their sound, the same C# which is quiet but incessant. No one else will ever hear it, there is no more air and the sound is locked inside your head, impossible to release by speaking or singing or even pounding the ground or trees or whistling through grass.

The memory of this dream is locked inside you, as is the dream itself. The sound of both is one whining note, could it be the same note that Cicero described in the *Somnium Scipionis?* Do you dream in tempered tones? Is your pitch secure, even when asleep? Or only when asleep?

Experience of singing is for you an auditory one, you have never sung aloud. You cannot remember doing so, at least. Singing while asleep is possible, even beautiful, the pitch is perfect and breathing effortless. Nevertheless, no sound emerges during such performances. The breath you exhale is suspended, little bubbles escape as from a swimmer but there is no room for air, the space inside is completely full with nothing, and motionless. When you wake, breathing is normal but awkward. Your throat is scratchy as if from yelling. Glycerin is useful in lubricating your unused vocal chords. You have been under water a long time.

A Misunderstanding

Not wanting to be misunderstood, Cain never spoke again. These words, being unpronounced, were therefore the holiest of all the words of the ancient fathers. His people multiplied in silence. In their villages nothing was said. Ultimately the tribe of Cain lost the ability to speak, as knowledge of language disappeared over time. Much later, a young generation began to make noises. Not speech, but grunts or groans. Also high-pitched shrieks. A neighboring tribe was drawn to the sounds, and discovered there a pack of animals they had never before seen. Unsure of their origin, the neighboring tribe debated as to whether these creatures were divine or demonic. They argued for days. At last the wisest man in the tribe declared that divine or demonic, these creatures were dangerous. Their intent could not be understood. And so the neighboring tribe slaughtered the tribe of Cain, erasing their bodies from the Earth just as their language had long ago disappeared, completing the punishment God had chosen for them in the time of the ancient fathers; and condemning themselves to the same future fate.

The Envelope

The envelope was an unprecedented invention; for in those days nothing was hidden from view, the occult was as yet unborn, even metaphors of obstruction and enclosure were unknown. It is true that people wore clothes, but they did not carry wallets — and the letters they wrote were transported by hand, out in the open, from place to place.

A room with doors was considered uncomfortable, not bad luck because, as has already been suggested, luck had then only a positive connotation. The ear was considered the organ closest to the seat of emotion, representing the openness of the body to the influences of the world. To have an occluded ear, or to be hard of hearing, was considered the greatest handicap.

When people wrote letters, they sat at desks without

drawers, before windows without curtains. These letters were not the sorts of direct personal address with which we are now familiar. They were, as befitted their different material existence, open addresses to the society at large. The author of a letter would just as soon hand it to an unfamiliar party as deliver it to someone he or she knew. This ambiguity of recipient caused the author no consternation during the letter's composition.

Eventually letters came to be published for all to read at once. These books of letters had no covers, nor were they "bound" in the sense we would use the word today. Their exact form is difficult for us to picture concretely. However we know they were read, alone or in groups, in both private and public settings, not least of which were the baths.

This was the world into which the inventor of the envelope was born. The delivery, legend tells us, was witnessed only by the mother. Out of her womb came the entire amniotic sac, unbroken, opaque but with a definite form within. The alarmed woman raised the sac to the light, transfixed by a series of mysterious emblems in the blood vessels of the enclosure.

Reading

Opening a book, at random. This book, if it so happens, but the likelihood is small. Because of all readers, how many will ever read a particular book. And then, of all particular books, how often might one choose the one being written. Perhaps in the stars a knowledgeable person could foresee, or at least explain the likelihood. A perfect problem for the stars, of reconciling the universe (readers) with the internal (writing). Or it could be rephrased: reconciling the public with the private. But now we've asserted that writing is private, which, by immediately associating it with reading, we had already contradicted. Writing is public. Reading is private. And thus this book, having been written in public, is being read in private. Unless you are reading in a public place, but that is beside the point. Isn't it? Because in your public place you are being private, reading. Or you are reading aloud. But what is the likelihood of that. Very little.

Reading aloud is a confusion of the private (reading) with the public (aloud), another problem for the stars; or more accurately, a problem only to be solved by those with the right strengths and weaknesses in their charts. For the rest it is an embarrassment. Where you are doesn't matter. That is the point. That is why the stars can answer literary questions. This is an oblique point, but its chance of being true is none the less for it. Of all statements, most have the same likelihood of being true. Even the most outrageous statements of fact — all is made of water, for example — have a good chance of being true. Why then is it so hard to write the truth? It is not hard to read the truth. In fact it is a pleasure. But writing it is painful and perhaps impossible. It should follow that reading the truth is likewise impossible, except that one can read falsehoods and take them as truth. Reading is a transformative process. Writing is not. The writer is unchanged from the start of a book to the finish. Even Augustine, saved before he starts his account of sin. But reading? The reader is always different at the end of the book than at the beginning. The reader is changing constantly.

The writer is reactionary. And perhaps this is the reason why a given book has only the slimmest chance of being opened at any particular time. Because the book never changes, and the reader constantly does. Time, which of course always changes, it is the tritest of statements to write, is the reader's element. And the writer is uncomfortable with time, the writer's book is uncomfortable with time, everything the writer does indicates the writer's discomfort with time. But the reader? If a book has a reader, as this one now does, it is manipulated in time by that reader, as if it didn't have any other existence. Which it doesn't, as a work being read. As a work having been written, it is an artifact of the past. As anything else, only the reader might say. What do you say? Of course you cannot tell the writer. Long gone, the writer. Or at some unreachable distance. Or, worse yet, if you are to meet the writer, completely uninterested in learning what you have to say, and even more repulsive, uninteresting himself. Most are egotistical and boring, to boot. Clichés and self-importance, those are the writer's elements. And self-pity. And a consuming ambition to write. Even to write what isn't necessary. Because what is necessary? The truth. And no one writes the truth. The writer writes drivel and falsehoods, and the reader reads beauty and truth. Do you not? Perhaps some readers read ugliness and lies. But how would one read ugliness and lies? As truth. That is the point already made. Writers are repetitious and self-referential. This is because they have nothing to write. It is likely that you have already gathered that. You read that truth long ago in the lies that you were presented. Long ago in this book (which is not yet long, but you have no reason to think it won't be, like all other books, too long) or long ago in your reading of other books. This cannot be the first book you have ever read. If so, this is an absurd situation. Of all possible readers, reading all possible books, the likelihood that this book is being read at all is slim, and the likelihood of it being read as the reader's first book ever is even slimmer, if not outright impossible. Because readers begin with books that pretend to tell the truth, but are full of lies. Fairy tales, stories for children, all filled with self-conscious lies but presented as the truth. Here you have a different case, one to be encountered only later, after having read a number of books. This is the case of a book telling lies and only lies. No pretense to truth. You however will read some truth into this. But the writer cannot know for sure. Perhaps, at some distance in time or space or merely psychic distance introduced by the character of one who reads, and perhaps also writes, but who is at this moment primarily a reader not a writer, this book will be read for what it is, which is lies. And then perhaps reading will be something other than predicted here. However that would confirm that this book tells lies, or at least falsehoods. This is the sort of repulsive self-reflexivity that is typical of writing. And books are useless for this reason. Useless to anyone but readers.

In Private

It is necessary to write this because I have forgotten who I am. I can look in the mirror, but that only reacquaints me with my image; it is the same with photographs. I have spoken and sung into a tape recorder, and have heard my voice. I have looked through all my papers, and rediscovered my social history. I can remember all the details of my personal life. But my private thoughts I cannot recall.

It is possible that I have never had any private thoughts. However, in that case I do not know why I suddenly feel that I should have them.

Therefore I am writing to conjure my private thoughts, or at least to establish why I feel they are missing.

It is also possible that I have had private thoughts

before, and written them down, and lost them. That would account both for their absence and my familiarity with their existence. In this case I am perhaps now beginning to reconstruct them. The first private thought, it seems, would be the need for private thoughts.

That might explain this page of writing. But what would a second private thought be?

I now realize that I have written this page before. I have written this page thousands of times, and thrown it away. That is why it was not among my personal papers. I have had this one private thought all my life — that I have no private thoughts — and written it down time and again, hoping it would lead to another. But it never does.

After the Tempest

An opera would be a good sequel, primarily because the dramatic problems of a sequel are avoided by the undramatic form of aria, aria, aria: all lyric. But the story becomes a simple comedy — Prospero, the worried father, marries off his daughter and the final chorus is sung by all. The book is drowned, but in rhyme. No mention of a staff.

Sleep

IT IS NOW KNOWN that the best measure of life is not years and months and days, but cumulative hours of sleep. Each body is granted a finite amount of sleep, which may be divided in any manner. Those craving more life have taken outrageous measures to remain awake, but such behavior seems to rarely, if ever, prolong a body's age beyond the old average expectations. More successful have been those craving death, an ever-larger group of dedicated sleepers who consider each waking hour time wasted, and time asleep as bliss, both peace and progress. There is a religious fervor to these sleepers, who chant themselves to sleep with monotonous prayers of time's end. There are, finally, the sensualist sleepers, who savor each moment asleep like sips from a precious bottle of wine. Unappreciated minutes of sleep are to them an unthinkable waste, and dreams are valued as incomparable visions of truth. It is these sleepers, wreathed in incense, wrapped in silk pajamas, and cultivating exotic herbal, alcoholic, and pharmacological practices to better stimulate their attentive moments of unconsciousness, who will write the history of sleeping life. They are after all the only ones who still allow themselves to read — a dangerously soporific activity for those who never want to sleep, and a pointless one for those who do.

Read Me

One of the problems with death, for the intellectual classes, is that it leaves so many unfiled and perhaps unwanted papers in its wake. I carefully arranged all my papers — destroying those I do not want to survive me, organizing for a stranger's eye all others — and thus prepared to die, at least from an organizational point of view. However I continued to live, generating more papers, which threatened to survive me in a form I had not prepared. Therefore I have now made final arrangements, and will live my remaining days without paper or pencil. It may be that I die for lack of a writing implement — if I need to send an urgent message to someone for help, for example — but this statement will remain the last in my file, the first to greet the executors. For all they know, I am still alive. If so, it is however a paperless existence, and therefore moot in terms of my legacy.

To Levitate

WAKING UP in complete darkness (hotel bed in an alcove), I remembered that — as a child — I had the power to levitate. Now the ability came to me in a dream when, for various reasons, I needed to leap across a body of water. Suddenly I remembered the key to my abilities: focus on the arrival of my feet on the ground just ahead, constantly moving that point forward, thereby prolonging my step indefinitely. Never concentrate on the levitation. Just the step that doesn't end.

When did I lose my ability to levitate? Between my parents' arms, leaning on them as I moved my feet over the ground without touching. On an escalator in a department store, lifting myself above the treads. In an airport on a moving sidewalk, floating above the ground that stood still.

Now the crocodiles and menacing sea lions of a

mountain resort threaten my biologist friend and myself. It is true that forgotten powers reawaken when necessary. The mountains are themselves forbidding, which I tell my friend. Her lack of fear inspires my endless leap. Thank you friend! And the monsters are so disappointed, I see it in their eyes.

Mildred Pierce

What happened was that as Mildred's expanded, the food we were asked to eat was just too much, too fast. At first it was a pleasure; the fried chicken, in particular. We sat at checkered tablecloths and were careful not to spill the gravy or make crumbs — the set dressers were vigilant, and among the meanest people at the studio. The coffee was good, too, very hot, but we were not permitted to blow on it because this action distended our cheeks, and consequently many burned their mouths, without grimacing of course.

But the plot called for more Mildred's, more chicken, more scalding coffee, and also those mile-high cream pies, the kind no one makes anymore, as if they were prohibited. Why not make a pie so tall it cannot fit anywhere but a Hollywood set? But even the pies began to wear on us. The variety helped — pumpkin, apple, and the myriad creams:

pineapple, banana, lemon chiffon — however many of us began to fall ill. Those who fell sick nonetheless showed up for work, because work was not plentiful, and in addition to our wages we were eating well; but the eating was difficult enough without feeling sick.

Then we had to travel, to the Mildred's at Laguna Beach, to the many Mildred's in the booming Valley — often in one day, at one meal even. The script would call for chickens down south and pie back north. The choice assignment was Beverly Hills, but soon they stopped serving food there altogether and used it only for the office scenes. While Mildred was working in Beverly Hills, we were eating everywhere else, keeping the money flowing, the business booming. The plot necessities were clear, but none of us could see how it could last.

And it didn't last. Not enough mouths, not enough chicken, not enough pie to pay for all the costs associated with the now ubiquitous Mildred's. An entire population was eating, but it wasn't enough. It would take the end of the war, returning soldiers, big new families, to eat all the food this plot required. Before that could happen they killed off the principals, closed the set, put us out of work. Then we missed the chicken and coffee. I remember arguments about which Mildred's had been the best, which pie, which gravy with the fried chicken. These were long, impassioned bouts of nostalgia for a set the likes of which we would never see again, food we could only recall in black and white, that looked so good we could never be sure we had ever really tasted it.

The Extra

At a certain point in life one ceases to be oneself, and from that moment forward one chooses one's own personality, which is necessarily someone else's. This is not a moment to be sanguine about one's past. It is, rather, a moment when one must focus all one's energies on the question at hand, and make the right decision.

In my new role as extra, I have no role at all, but only a presence. My character may be someone else's, but without a character of my own there is no way to distinguish between them. The lie of my being may therefore be avoided: truth is possible, in the absence of substance.

The extra was seen in the background, maybe acting badly. But in the foreground was the deception, the big lie. The background is only a set piece, a hint of time and place. Flats lifted away and stored after the performance. Scrims hoisted dramatically into the flies...

When Hart Crane jumped into the painting of the sea, he did indeed drown. Extras jump and jump and jump, and never fall more than a few feet, into bales of hay. The hay is scratchy, and its smell is of the barnyard. Extras are rolling in it.

The Secret Museum

THE HORN ON the Victrola looked inviting, so I jumped inside. It was cool, and smooth to the touch. I fell, but slowly, and so I was not afraid. I became very small; I believe the force of my fall influenced my shape, which began to conform to the inside of the horn. Eventually I became a single point. And I entered the groove of a record, which launched me as pure sound. A vibration. I carry no melody, not even a note. My transfiguring moment fell between beats, and so I am an aspect of that atmospheric scratch in the background. Before me, and after me, came the most beautiful trumpet solo.

Hearts and Pearls
(or, the lounge lizard's lost love)

WHAT SEEMED obvious on arrival is now obscure and giving me a headache. The dialogue cards call for tender words. But tenderness, what is tenderness, and what tenderness can I hope to speak while falling from a height into a bank of snow? I might as well put guitars on my feet and clomp around, as attempt to sing. I might as well walk through snow with guitars on my feet, as sing.

Where sharpshooters plot devilish crimes, there I'll be, tucked in a corner, scribbling away at some poorly conceived attempt at exposé. Knock me on the head, why don't you, while I try to write this. Or walk through the room dressed like that, it's the same thing. Give me odds; I'll take a shot at myself too.

When we finally get together, I'll whisk you away to a mail-order house, we can both work in shipping and tangle up the wires. I could make breakfast at the bottom of the sea for you. I could swim through the aisles. I could float like an anchor.

What love is, I suspect, comes in these numbered boxes. But it is as if they have been reordered, all my feelings come out wrong, or rather in the wrong sequence. My proposal, finally, is unpacked, but you left long ago when the trial separation interrupted the honeymoon. You have been back, it is true, at holidays. And hasn't my cooking improved, now that the stove has been moved indoors?

Nothing mocks success like more of it. I could somersault I am so happy. But I am so sad I turn cartwheels straight off a cliff.

Caresse Crosby Dreams a Dream

My daughters at my side dressed in pinafores. The man just off the *Lusitania* at the dock, poem in hand: "We will sew our lips together…"

Let me present an opium vision, a memory from that room with four bathtubs, the view over the Seine and me, naked, illuminated to a cheering *Bateau-Mouche*. In the dream one says yes or no, and I choose yes. So we were married in an Inca ceremony officiated by a student sculptor who suffocated us in wet clay. What choice is left me? What instruction or command?

I try to follow my deceased companion. His taxi is too quick and the driver makes rude gestures at the passers-by.

At the hotel it is none too romantic, though management has thoughtfully neglected to remove the previous occupants' caviar tins. They are blue and black and intricately stamped with impressions of fish scales. I contemplate my journey in the mirror. My relatives in Boston telegram for my arrest. Later that evening, back on Beacon Hill, the guests shiver at my negligée, carved in champagne ice. Who asked whom, I toss off, wet feet on carpet making my bobbed hair stand on end. Fear is a poem I burned, wrapping its ashes in silk, and ate like meringue.

Ghosts

Six ghosts were in my house last night. They sat smoking in a corner, speaking their strange language, occasionally translating the best jokes for me. They opened the windows, but smoked so much I thought I would choke. I emptied ashtray after ashtray, and they smoked and smoked.

Later, they played music — but so loud! The tallest one, in white robes, sang, and ground a screeching hurdy-gurdy. The strongest played the drums, like he would kill them; he had been tattooed from head to foot by the one who played bass, who was also tattooed, with crosses and other, unfamiliar signs. One stood very still, and made strangling sounds with his guitar. Another tapped little bells, and stared at the sky as if in prayer. And one just danced about, shrieking and shaking a soundless tambourine.

These ghosts are my friends. They stayed in my

house another night. It was difficult having six smoking ghosts in my house, but when they left, I told them: next time, please bring more.

Mise en Abyme

I was overwhelmed by the size and variety of the world, and resolved to limit my interests to myself. However my self turned out to be more various than I had hoped. My history, for example, does not begin with my birth, or even my parents' births, but leaks out into an endless tree of personalities, cultures, and events. This is only considering the few generations I can trace. Beyond these I can only conjecture; an effort that requires the stockpiling of tremendous amounts of information.

Geography is likewise problematic. The street on which I was born, for example, has had many occupants, both commercial and residential. Researching a simple list of these occupants has proven to be a task worthy of years' labor. And obviously this is only one street, I have walked on many streets in my day.

Which brings me to the paradox of this self-interested hobby. Each day I add to the events which need examination. Completion is impossible, for — to take the most extreme but perhaps most telling example — even the moment of completion would require its own notation, and that moment further notation, etcetera.

It is clear from my failures that the self is not an appropriate subject for study. (This is the only conclusion I can draw from a lifetime of self-examination.)

When I met Lewis Carroll he said to me, "As a fact, suicide is not interesting. But as a theory, it invites consideration of an ancient figure: the serpent swallowing its tail. A person ridding the world of him or herself is an infinite regression, and any act that partakes of the infinite is a candidate for the spiritual, the godly, for perfection."

Only One Thing is Missing

We are a mysterious island, whose contours must be mapped and named, resources catalogued and exploited, animals captured and domesticated; whose rivers must be bridged, harbors secured, and caverns explored; wool carded, oysters seeded, herbs collected; lakes lowered (by dynamite) and raised again (by means of a dam); ropes woven, ladders constructed, lifts contrived; apes befriended, servants trained; ...and at whose core there exists some power, whose presence is made known only in times of danger, and whose purpose is the preservation of this island and its hierarchy of existence.

The Blue God

Nostalgic for a time of saints and mesmerists, I took up residence in Lynn, Massachusetts, near the house once occupied by Mary Baker Eddy. Lynn is the grimmest of towns, despite its location near the magnificent Massachusetts coastline. And it has always been the sort of awful place that attracts saints and mesmerists.

It was for this reason that I was not overly surprised to find the Blue God in Lynn. I saw him first in a photograph by Wallace Nutting, taken at a picturesque bend in a road, shaded by great chestnut trees. The photo, hand-colored, I found in a junk shop. Nutting's photos are always hand-colored, but this one contained a speck of uncharacteristic blue. On closer inspection, I found a tiny figure underneath the chestnut trees, almost obscured by the brush overtaking some recently abandoned farmland…

I didn't meet the Blue God until some time later. The photo is hanging over my desk as I write this. The blue figure has since faded from view, I do not know if it is because of the sunlight at my back or the presence of the god himself.

When we did meet, the Blue God was no longer blue. He had been in the sun, like the photo. It was a very still day, and I had wandered down to the ocean. As I stood at the shore, before a perfectly flat sea, I had the sensation that the water was solid. Nothing moved: there were no waves, or birds, or boats. In retrospect I have realized that I was witness to a rare moment of cosmological inertia. And suddenly he was there, striding along the beach. He was announcing, I now believe, the moment of rest.

When he was once again in the distance, precisely the size of the figure in the Nutting photo, I saw him turn to blue.

Meditation

Were one able to recall the precise moment one falls asleep, the thoughts revealed during that instant would produce complete peace, both for the singularly alert sleeper and the world at large; for the message hidden in that moment would, once revealed, be recognized instantly by every person as the very thought that has forever eluded their consciousness, and is ineluctably right.

In hopes of discovering this universally forgotten thought, I have stayed awake for fifty years, and what was once an exercise in meditation and self-abnegation that drove me to the brink of enlightenment has now become insomnia.

Nevertheless the continual occupation of this same spiritual ground that I once held so devoutly has, regardless of my increasing cynicism, deepened my understanding of the fact of spirituality, if not its content. It is this knowledge that I wish to communicate to the world, now that I recognize I will never know the message I originally set out to discover.

That spirituality is a fact can be demonstrated simply by my existence, that is, simply by existence itself. Anything, if it sits long enough, will meditate; and anything, once meditating, will progress toward a state of spirituality; and anything that lasts is, therefore, spiritual at least in some degree. I myself have outlasted usefulness, and my life has illustrated this theorem by gaining in spirituality what it has lost in meaningfulness. Its meaning has become its spirituality, a dangerous development that could lead to a further logical loss in spirituality, and consequently in meaning, and so on unto nothingness; but this nothingness would no doubt be the enlightenment I once felt so close I kissed its cheek with my eyelash.

However, enlightenment comes only once per life, if at all, and its retreat is final. In its wake is existence — precisely what I thought I might escape (the same thought that drove away its shadow, no doubt) — and in existence is bright light, incessant noise, insomnia.

Insomnia is forever, and it has lent me its permanence, with which I have gained said spirituality through endurance. And so I endure, awake, to tell you these thoughts, truths learned in a dream I had once fifty years ago and which frightened me so severely I have yet to sleep again.

A Parable
(my wanderjahre)

They stole all my clothes, and so I stood naked in the department store, waiting for service. Commanded to sing, I could only remember fight songs from a college I never attended. They put rings on my fingers, and draped me in furs. I was forced to eat caviar with small portions of sour cream, or perhaps it was *crème fraîche,* I could not know having never tasted *crème fraîche.* It was announced in the newspapers that I was a child of kings. My feet were anointed, I have no idea with what. Incense was burning when I passed out near the altar. Coming to, I heard a choir of little boys. I was to eat only round foods: eggs, potatoes, oranges, beans. If I admired my furs, I was to roll in the mud. There was a flooded river, and I was swept away. Caught on a branch, I escaped the falls. The branch broke, but the river stood still. My furs dried without a stain. I walked to the top of the highest mountain.

The Argument

Is it that my memories have run out? Or is it the potential for creating memories that has been exhausted?

Or is memory an object, something given to you by another, outside the Museum of Natural History for example, on a cold day when there is no school?

Can these objects, once assimilated, become one's own, or do they remain gifts from those we have forgotten? Does the giver of a gift disappear, his or her presence dissolved into the gift itself? Or is it the purpose of the gift that disappears?

What remains is not anyone, and not anything, but the sense of things given by someone forgotten. These are memories, and thus not knowing anyone or receiving anything brings a halt to their production.

The Image

The image enters your life in an unobtrusive manner, buries itself under the skin, and resurfaces at a moment of lightheartedness. But then it turns and burrows so deep it can no longer be seen, or, if seen, is unrecognizable. In a dream it reemerges: chimera-like, it is comprised of the many images with which it has since come into contact. Clinging to its edges, like seaweed, and to its surface like barnacles, are the strings and cankers of fear and anxiety. Its face is horrible. Its absorption is now complete, and irrevocable. You are made up of such images, you encounter new ones at a tremendous rate...

Poetry

Even if religion and song are the distillation of a people's collective imagination, there are some things for which the individual alone must be responsible. And for these things there is no explanation. Why should Ganesh, whose elephant head I am willing to assign to the genius of a people, be greeted by an arrhythmic crash of cymbals whenever he enters the stage of the Ramayana play? This detail is too trivial for the imagination of an entire people. I must assign it instead to that lone percussionist, genius or imbecile, whose momentary success initiated a tradition. Surprise cannot emanate from a people, whose individual imaginations are calibrated to one another through myth and faith. The imagination may rule our waking and dreaming lives, but impulse — perhaps it is only impulse — remains the domain of personal irrationality. A religion or song based on irrationality would be incomprehensible, it would in no way mirror our imaginations, which are as orderly as they are fantastic. Fantasy is itself predictable and rigid, like those set entertainments through which we all suffered as children. Irrationality, by contrast, mirrors our individual souls. In it we recognize ourselves, but never our friends, relations, or neighbors — it therefore makes poor material for religions and songs — and is the only possible material for poetry.